The Care and Keeping of Customers

The Care and Keeping of Customers

A Treasury of Facts, Tips, and Proven Techniques for Keeping Your Customers Coming BACK!

Roy Lantz

SkillPath Publications
Mission, KS

Project Editor: Kelly Scanlon

Editor: Jane Doyle Guthrie

Page Layout: Premila Malik Borchardt, Rod Hankins

Cover Design: Rod Hankins, Steve Shamburger

Cover Illustration: Ron Wheeler

Library of Congress Catalog Card Number: 95-74669

ISBN: 1-57294-007-7

10 9 8 7 6 5 4 3 2   97 98 99

Contents

Introduction

$\mathcal{D}$o you ever have the sinking feeling that certain businesses should display a sign—just like the one above Hell's gate in Dante's *Inferno*—that says "Abandon hope, all ye who enter here"? From Altoona, Pennsylvania, to Abu Dhabi, United Arab Emirates, the endless variety of customer service horror stories that people are ready to share is consistently amazing!

Although these incredible tales alone could easily fill volumes, this book has a very different goal—to help you ensure that your customers remain *your* customers. You will learn proven techniques and concepts to help you avoid that most distressing of all customer behaviors—taking business elsewhere. You'll also have the opportunity to experience hands-on exercises that help you identify the characteristics of great service and great service providers.

The White House Council on Consumer Affairs several years ago set out on a research project that continues to have profound implications for customer service. The Council discovered that, depending on industry, market area, demographics, and so forth, it can cost five to six times more to get a new customer than it costs to keep one you already have. The message here is loud and clear, isn't it?

Certainly most of us can't survive in business without adding new customers. However, if new customers are the lifeblood of a business, then current customers are the heart that keeps that lifeblood flowing! In other words, you want customers who'll come BACK—and that provides a useful acronym for the four key elements to making sure they do:

*B*ehaviors

*A*ttitudes

*C*ommunication

*K*nowledge

Each of the four major chapters in this book tackles one of these areas in detail.

Implementing as many of the ideas suggested in these chapters as you can will keep your organization's heart healthy and alive. There's nothing quite as gratifying as knowing that you have earned a customer's repeat business—that you have given a customer a reason to come back to you. Throughout this book, you'll learn the behaviors, the attitudes, the communication techniques, and the knowledge required to deliver exceptional service that delights customers on a consistent basis. Approach these techniques with an open mind, invest the time required to do the exercises, and you'll be well underway to the successful care and keeping of your customers!

Chapter One

Behaviors That Stand Out to Customers

"If you're not serving the customer, you'd better be serving someone who is."
—*Karl Albrecht and Ron Zemke in Service America*

$\mathcal{C}$an you finish this familiar sentence?

"Actions speak _____   _____
_____."

That was easy, wasn't it? Everyone knows that "actions speak louder than words." We're familiar with that saying because it's so very true, but it's also often familiar *by its absence* in customer service.

Several years ago UCLA professor Albert Mehrabian, one of America's leading communications experts, published a landmark study in identifying how we communicate. After thousands of hours of exhaustive research, Dr. Mehrabian's work documented the validity of "actions speak louder than words" quite conclusively. And the results were startling—when speaking to another, our entire message is interpreted this way:

- 7 percent of what is heard are the words (verbal)
- 38 percent of what is heard is voice tone (vocal)
- 55 percent of what is heard is body language (visual)

The implications of this in customer service are enormous. If you are to be believed when apologizing to customers, or explaining why a policy serves their best interest, you must pay particular care to *how* you say what you say. In other words, your *behaviors*, far more than your words, will determine what a customer really hears.

As you read this, you may be thinking, "Well, I'm not a front-line service person, so I don't know that these data really apply to me." But as the quote from Karl Albrecht and Ron Zemke at the beginning of this chapter most emphatically states, this information applies to everyone in the organization. Even if you aren't a front-line provider, your behavior, *no matter what your role in the organization,* will ultimately have an impact on front-line people, and therefore on the customer.

Let's take a look now at some business behaviors that make a big difference where customers are concerned.

Remember to use "policy" as bridges, not barriers.

Which of the following phrases do you think is deadlier for a customer to hear: "It's not my job!" or "It's against company policy!" Though you may be surprised, "It's against company policy!" is far worse than passing the buck. Why? Because "It's not my job!" leaves open the *possibility* of service, since it implies that the matter is *somebody's* job (and therefore there's hope for a solution).

A great example of the potentially devastating impact of "policy" appeared some time ago in a *Wall Street Journal* article. The article told of a gentleman who visited his bank in New York to cash a small personal check and asked that his parking ticket be validated. The teller explained the bank *policy* that cashing a personal check "was not considered a banking transaction" and, therefore, she could not validate the parking ticket.

Understandably questioning such "policy," the gentleman asked to see the manager, who immediately parroted the teller, emphasizing that this "was not considered a banking transaction." The gentleman then asked if he might write one more check. After receiving a condescending "Certainly" from the manager, the gentleman wrote a check for nearly two million dollars, withdrawing all his money from the bank. Before going across the street to open a new account, he was overheard asking the manager, "Does this constitute a banking transaction?"

Policy should be a *bridge* that allows you to cross over to the customer, allows the customer to cross over to you, and, when necessary, lets you meet somewhere in between. All too often, though, policy becomes a formidable *barrier* to service excellence. If you have a policy that confuses employees, inconveniences customers, or worse, both, that policy needs to be seriously reevaluated.

"Because we've always done it this way" is not in itself sufficient reason to do it this way now!

"If it ain't broke, fix it anyway."

About 96 percent of unhappy customers won't tell you they're unhappy. This rather alarming fact comes from the same White House Council report cited earlier. Do you know what's really scary about that statistic? It's the fact that these folks won't tell *you* they're unhappy. Who, then, will they tell? They'll tell *everybody else*—friends, neighbors, even people they've just met. And if positive word-of-mouth is one of the best ways to attract new business, you can be sure the testimony of an unhappy customer is one of the best ways to repel it!

Welcome complaints.

It's hard to imagine anybody in business saying "Wow, I really love complaints!" But consider that of the 96 percent of unhappy customers mentioned in Tip #2, 91 percent will go elsewhere if their dissatisfaction isn't resolved. So, although you may never learn to love 'em, you most definitely must learn to welcome complaints if your goal is consistent service excellence at the highest levels. Complaints serve as opportunities to keep your customers *your* customers!

4

High tech is no longer enough; "high touch" is the key for success in today's competitive markets.

There was a time, not that long ago, when the "playing field" of customer service was not as level as it is today. Some organizations, because of their size and apparently limitless resources, had access to remarkable technologies that the "little guys" just couldn't top. (In fact, it was this disparity in technology that caused some of the "little guys" to become so successful—they had to make up the difference with plain old-fashioned *service!*)

Today, thankfully, everyone has greater access to the technologies that allow surer, more responsive customer service. That's the good news. The bad news is that far too many organizations now rely on technology—the "high tech" of customer service—while disregarding the people side of the equation—the "high touch." How many times have you found yourself lost in the labyrinth of an electronic phone system (in place, no doubt, in the name of increased efficiency)?

Avoid making negative comments about your competition.

Here's a true story: Mike had purchased a pleasure boat from a particular dealer and decided a few years later to give that dealer the opportunity to sell him a newer (and far larger, more expensive) craft. From the moment he entered the showroom and casually made a flattering remark about a boat at a competing dealership, he was assaulted with negative and most unflattering assertions about the competing dealership *and* their boats! The verbal barrage halted only long enough for other "salespeople" to join in on the attack.

What on earth could these people have been thinking? What was their point? Mike hurriedly left the showroom, checkbook *closed* and firmly in hand, and went down the street to the other dealership. There he happily wrote a large check for what was really his *second choice* boat. He was not going to reward the behavior at that first dealership. Would you?

⟨6⟩

Most dissatisfied customers will return if handled properly and quickly.

According to the Technical Assistance Research Project of the White House Council on Consumer Affairs, somewhere between 54 and 70 percent of unhappy customers will do business with you again if their complaint is handled properly. That figure jumps to an amazing 95 percent if it's handled properly *and quickly.* You need only recall your personal experiences as a customer to verify that assertion!

7

Whenever possible, offer warranties, guarantees, and other solid assurances.

One of the biggest causes of service failure is the tendency to overpromise, because this inevitably results in *underdelivery*. And underdelivery doesn't have to occur in reality—the *perception* is all it takes. Consider a service guarantee only if you can consistently ensure service at the highest level.

Although a well-thought-out service guarantee is one of the strongest statements you can make about your commitment to service, many organizations are reluctant to offer one because of fear of abuse. Rest assured, however, that such fears are generally unfounded—most people just want what they came for.

You'll probably find that a really strong guarantee will mean more to your employees—your *internal* customers—than it does to those who purchase your product or service. The message such a guarantee sends is clear: You believe in your employees' ability to deliver.

⌒ 8 ⌒

Only a fraction of customers will leave because of price; most will leave because of indifference.

Occasionally you will lose business because of pricing, but the Technical Assistance Research Project report cited in Tip #6 says that it happens only in about 9 percent of lost-business incidents. Fully 68 percent of customers—almost seven of ten—leave because of perceived *indifference* on the part of the company they were dealing with!

If asked, "Are you indifferent to your customers?" your response most assuredly would not be, "Oh yeah, I don't really care about 'em." But whether *you* feel you are indifferent or not, the real issue is *"What is your customers' perception?"* Perception is reality as far as they're concerned. You may think you are providing service at the highest level, but if your customer doesn't feel that way, then you're really not, are you? Service, like beauty, is in the eye of the beholder.

Consider the characteristics of truly exceptional customer service by asking yourself the following three questions. Or, as an alternative, try working through them with other members of your team—you'll not only elicit a variety of ideas, but the exercise will leave a far greater impression than any lecture or pep talk could.

1. Where do you go to get "Wow!!" service? This level of service is difficult to describe, yet incredibly easy to recognize (because it's so rare)—you'll pay more for it, you'll drive out of your way to get it, and you'll wait longer for it, yet precious few places offer it.

2. What are the specific characteristics—what are the behaviors—that make the service at those places so exceptional?

3. Can your organization offer these characteristics? Even more important, how?

A close partner to Behavior in the service realm is *Attitude*, the second vital component in keeping customers coming BACK. The next chapter will focus on developing a winning service attitude in your organization.

Chapter Two

Attitudes of Exceptional Service

"Customer service is an attitude, not a department."

*T*hat opening quote, or some variation of it, is probably familiar to you. It puts things comfortably in a nutshell, so maybe you've never questioned what it's really saying. But think about it—*what is attitude?*

It is simply the way you choose to respond. "Choose? What choice?" you say. "I can't control a customer who won't listen to reason or a boss who just doesn't understand." No, you can't control all situations, but you can control your response. And that's all attitude is: choosing *your* response.

Facing a hostile, irate, and belligerent customer? (Not a pretty picture, is it?) You can *choose* not to match that behavior. Have a boss who talks about customer service, but doesn't show real commitment? To the extent that you are able, you can *choose* service excellence for yourself.

This chapter examines more than a dozen of the core components necessary for getting customers to consistently come BACK, the *attitudes* of exceptional service.

⌐ 9 ⌐

Find out how your customers want to be treated—not necessarily how you want to be.

One of the things that makes being on this planet truly marvelous also makes customer service a truly marvelous opportunity—no two people are exactly alike. And though the Golden Rule is a great guideline, you must not assume that everyone always wants to be treated the way you want to be. What's the best way to find out how customers want to be treated? *Ask!* (In Chapter 3, "Communication Techniques That Work," you'll examine a number of practical ways to do so.)

⌁ **10** ⌁

Do sweat the small stuff—little things can mean a lot

How many times have you been told (or said yourself), "Don't sweat the small stuff"? What a handy little "rational lie," especially when the topic is customer service! The "small stuff" doesn't mean *extras* that you'd like to provide, but rather the details that *should* be a normal part of customer service, but are often overlooked.

For example, a professional trainer shared the following anecdote about audiovisual equipment services: "I can't tell you how many different overhead projectors I've used in the past year—*easily* 200 would be my guess. I *can* tell you how many times the glass surface of the projector was cleaned before it was presented for my use—twice! That's right, only about 1 percent of the time was the projector fully ready for use. Oh, it was ready 100 percent of the time before the presentation began, but 99 percent of the time I—the customer—was responsible for making it ready."

Think about the opportunities you have for "cleaning the glass" (or *sweating the small stuff*) in your service operation. Your competitors aren't doing it!

11

Empower employees to help without going through bureaucratic "channels."

A terrific example of the benefits of empowering employees (authorizing them to think) occurred some time ago at a Wichita, Kansas, branch of a major national retail chain. At the time, the chain itself and this store in particular were facing some major challenges in terms of market share. Closing this store was being considered as an option. The store manager, sensing there was very little to lose, empowered the front-line people to authorize returns, to okay checks, to approve refunds—in short, to do whatever it took to please the customer without going through time-consuming, frequently belittling "channels."

Did it work? Only if you consider a dramatic increase in business, a marked upswing in employee morale, a decrease in turnover and absenteeism, and greatly improved scores on customer satisfaction indices as success!

As you read this, you may be thinking: "Well, that's fine for a single store, or branch, or office, but what about us? We're a huge operation with dozens of locations and hundreds (or thousands!) of employees—*what about us?*"

A compelling response to that concern appears in the following "Policy Manual" from one of the country's most respected and fastest growing retail organizations, Nordstrom Department Stores:

Welcome to Nordstrom

We're glad to have you with our company.

Our number one goal is to provide outstanding customer service.

Nordstrom Rules:

Rule #1: Use your good judgment in all situations.

There will be no additional rules.

Now *that's* empowerment, but most of us don't see it shared to this extent in the typical business setting. In fact, individual empowerment is one of the biggest needs employees sense in most service organizations. Unfortunately, though, just like dissatisfied customers, employees don't communicate this to the people who can make a change. The general manager of a plastics manufacturing plant who had service responsibility throughout the Southeast found this out the hard way.

This manager knew he had as fine a team as he'd ever been associated with—including during his three years in the Marine Corps! He frequently wondered, however, why team members didn't approach him for more responsibility, more authority. When he left the company, he was saddened to learn the answer: Despite their excellent relationship with him, the members of the manager's front-line staff were quietly resentful that he didn't *give* them more responsibility and authority!

Don't let a lack of communicative *attitude* impair your efforts to achieve service excellence. Regardless of your position in the organization, try the following self-empowerment techniques:

- **Put it in writing.** You may have made suggestions, offered improvement ideas, or proposed alternative ideas in the past without much result. Putting your suggestions in writing, while guaranteeing nothing, will help them get attention.

- **Ask directly for what you want.** Remember, don't be quietly resentful that you're not getting more responsibility or authority; your boss may be wondering why you're not asking!

- **Set your own goals (and reward yourself).** Very few people get a lot of appreciation at work. When you've done well, let yourself (and others) know it!

Treat everyone, including employees, as a customer.

Have you noticed an increase in the number of organizations using the terms "internal customers" and "external customers"? IBM, for example, began to employ this concept some time ago. "Big Blue" has had its share of challenges, but the organization is coming back stronger and sounder than ever!

IBM recognized that without people to purchase their products and services, there would be no real need for the company! Since buyers (the external customers) were the folks with the money and resources to make the purchases, these people were identified as "Green Customers." At the same time, however, IBM recognized another profound truth of customer service—as much as the company relied on external customers to *purchase* their products and service, employees also had a strict reliance on each other (internal customers) to *provide* the products and services for purchase. Since the external (purchasing) customers were green, it was only natural to identify the internal (producing) IBM customers as blue!

The internal customer/external customer concept is a sound one, and you should consider using it in your organization.

13

Learn to say "I will," not "I'll try."

How often have you had a piece of luggage misplaced at the airport and been told, "We'll try to find it"? Or in response to a query concerning delivery been told, "We'll try to have it there tomorrow"? One of the great truths of customer service is that people do not care what you try to do—they want to know what you *will* do. There is always something you *can* do, if only to say, "I'll get back to you by 2:00 this afternoon." And what if it's 2:00 and you have nothing to report? Call anyway, to let the person know you're still working on it, and then arrange a specific time for another call.

At Human Resource Dynamics, a firm in Georgia, the staff has had success with what they call their "Sunset Scenario." This policy ensures that the business day will not end without the customer being informed of the current status of an unresolved issue. Try it—it works.

Commit to turning "irate" customers into "I rate!" customers.

Despite your best efforts, you will from time to time be confronted with an irate (or at best, dissatisfied) customer. Remember from Chapter 1, however, that no matter how upset the customer might be, *proper and prompt handling* can result in satisfaction up to 95 percent of the time.

So, is there a magic dust you can sprinkle or a phrase you can chant to cause this transformation? No, there's nothing mystical about it. Problem resolution just takes the following proven combination of *attitude* and *follow-through:*

- *Approach the situation professionally, not personally.* Affirm to yourself: "This is my job—I'm a professional. This person doesn't have to like me, and I don't have to like him or her."

- *Keep the focus on the issue and away from you.* Resolution of the complaint is the goal, not your "guilt" or "innocence" in the situation. And besides, have you ever heard of anyone ever winning an argument with a customer?

- *Be empathetic.* Express genuine concern. Let the customer know that what he or she is saying matters.

- *Uncover expectations.* What's the best way to do this? ASK! Question for clarity and understanding.

- **Lower your voice and slow down.** It's important that the customer perceives you as knowledgeable, authoritative, and in control. That perception diminishes, however, if your voice rises and you speak faster, as frequently happens in an angry customer scenario. So, be aware of your vocal quality.

- **Take notes on all essential information.** If you're meeting the customer in person, ask permission to take notes. On the telephone, do so automatically.

- **Repeat or, even better, paraphrase specifics.** Repeating and paraphrasing, though similar, are markedly different where customer service is involved. Repeating tells the customer you *heard* what was said; paraphrasing (saying back in *your own words* what was said) tells the customer you *listened.*

- **Outline possible solutions or alternatives.**
  "What can we do... ?"
  "Let's look at this together... "
  Avoid "I'll try." Say "I will."

- **Thank the customer for calling the issue to your attention.** Remember, 96 percent of unhappy customers won't tell you they're unhappy, and 91 percent of them simply take their business elsewhere.

- **Take action and follow up.** You and the customer have decided together what needs to be done. A decision to act is not enough, however. A final way to change "irate" to "I rate!" is to implement the decision and follow up to ensure that a win-win situation resulted.

⊂ 15 ⊃

Keep your attitude fine-tuned by reading books, listening to tapes, and attending programs on customer service.

The fact that you've invested in this book testifies that you are a customer service professional, committed to customer service excellence. Have you heard the old saying that if you continue to do what you're doing, you'll continue to get what you've got? *You* have obviously made the decision to grow personally and professionally, not to "continue to do what you're doing" but to do more.

If you can discipline yourself to read just fifteen minutes a day, five days a week (you don't have to grow on weekends!), you'll be investing nearly two weeks a year in your personal and professional growth—that's real time! At fifteen minutes daily, even if you're a slow reader, you could complete one to two books a month. Think how far ahead of the competition you'd be if you read a dozen or more books a year about customer service or the latest developments in your field.

⌒ 16 ⌒

Make "lagniappe" (that little something extra) a habit.

What on earth is *lagniappe,* how do you say it, and what does it have to do with customer service?!

Lagniappe (pronounced LAN-yap) sums up the essence of excellence in service—"that little something extra." It's a Cajun word from New Orleans, where grain traders included an extra shovelful of grain at no charge to the customer as a way of saying "thanks." More familiar, perhaps, would be the "baker's dozen" (though you don't see that much anymore, do you?). The giving of lagniappe is more than a "nice touch"; it's a signal to the customer that you care, and it's something *every* business can do. The following anecdote illustrates the concept memorably.

A traveling executive went down to the hotel lobby early in the morning to get a local paper. The front desk clerk said one would be available in the gift shop if it was open (it wasn't), or at the bell captain's stand. The bell captain informed him that the papers had not yet arrived, but that the vending machines on the corner were always serviced first and a paper would be available there. Before the executive could thank him, the bell captain added, "Would you like me to run down and get you one?" That's "that little something extra." Was the bell captain's offer a big deal? Of course not. Did it make a big impression? You bet!

☞ 17 ☜

Don't overpromise and build unrealistic expectations.

As stated in Tip #7, of all the well-meaning but deadly "attitudes" that prevail in customer service, overpromising is one of the most common. The good news is that it's also one of the easiest to avoid.

An excellent way to establish yourself in your market as one of the great customer service operations is to adopt a policy of *under*promising and *over*delivering. A delightful experience a colleague recently shared about a shoe repair shop will help explain this concept.

The fellow took a damaged travel bag to the shop for repair. The repairman said that he could easily fix it, that the job would be ready on Tuesday, and that the charge would be $13. Just as promised, the bag was ready on Tuesday, as good as new. The customer was prepared for that part—he was *expecting* it. What he wasn't expecting was the $9 invoice. The repairman explained that since he had the appropriate materials in stock, the repair didn't cost as much as he first thought it would.

Besides a like-new bag, that repairman engineered a customer for life!

⌐ 18 ⌐

Remember that management's attitude toward the customer will be copied.

"Don't do as I do, do as I say!" How many times did you hear that as a kid? Unfortunately, too many people in customer service continue to hear those nine dreadful words. Oh, the boss may not use *words* to convey it, but in so very many ways a message of *lip* service, not *customer* service, is sent to employees.

One of the hallmarks of the legends of exceptional service—the Federal Expresses, the Fairfield Inns, the Mary Kay Cosmetics—is management passion for customer service leadership through example.

ᴄ 19 ᴐ

Consider your customers as partners in your business.

How do you want to interact with your business partners? With mutual respect, free-flowing communication, shared visions, and a commitment to excellence, right? The results of such a partnership are powerful, particularly when you consider (and treat) your customers as part of the "loop." In a strong partnership you wouldn't hesitate to ask for input—nor should you hesitate to ask your customers. Most customers seem flattered, not offended, when you solicit their input. So ask!

✎ 20 ✎
See your business through the eyes of the customer.

Do you remember Flip Wilson's great line, "What you see is what you get!'"? Paraphrased just a bit, it's perfect for evaluating your organization's level of customer service— "What *you* see is what *they* get!" All too often we see our businesses, like our children, in a little different light than others do. Give the light switch one more "click"— turn it to bright, so you're looking at your business just as customers see it.

For example, you've been to the specialty shop where the owner is justifiably proud—the store is immaculate, the inventory is in order and impeccably displayed, and the atmosphere inside conveys a warm feeling. This is, of course, what she wants you to see as well, so outside there's a sign that reads:

<u>**NO**</u>

drinking

eating

smoking

strollers

If she'd turn the light up just a "click," she'd see that the sign is sending a different message than the one she intends. If she looked at it through her customers' eyes, she might change it to:

Please enjoy your food, drink, and "smokes" outside,

then come inside for one of our free smiles.

WELCOME AND ENJOY!

Do you see the difference? You know her customers do!

⌒ 21 ⌒

Make giving sincere compliments a habit.

The key word here obviously is *sincere*. There is nothing
as uplifting to a customer, internal or external, as a really
sincere compliment ("Thanks so much for waiting while I
took care of that phone call. I wish more little boys were
as patient and beautifully behaved as your little guy
there."). There's almost always something you can notice
and comment on positively, giving an extra "boost" to
each service encounter. There's also another plus to
making sincere complimenting a habit—every time you
give one, you feel better too!

⟨ 22 ⟩

Remember, service is defined by the supplier; satisfaction by the customer.

Have you ever been to a restaurant and things weren't quite the way you hoped they would be? You didn't have a *bad* experience necessarily; you just weren't really *satisfied* with everything. Your server, on the other hand, may have felt as though his or her performance represented the zenith of restaurant artistry! There was a big discrepancy, wasn't there, between his or her interpretation of the level of service and your level of satisfaction?

It matters very little what you, as a service provider, feel about your level of service; it's your customers' perception of the level of service that matters, and whether they feel satisfied.

Discrepancies like this can emerge when communication is allowed to falter. The next chapter delves into communication patterns and techniques, the third component to keeping customers coming BACK.

Chapter Three

Communication Techniques That Work

"The real art of conversation is not only to say the right thing in the right place but to leave unsaid the wrong thing at the tempting moment."
—Benjamin Franklin

Well said! Obviously, communication is much more than just conversation; in fact, the best definition is perhaps "the giving and getting of *understanding*." And the best way to do that? *Listen*. Former President Lyndon Johnson, while still in the Senate, kept the following sign on his desk, which summed up communicating succinctly, if not eloquently:

"When you're talkin', you ain't learnin'!"

Let's try something. Look at these scrambled letters—what word can you see if you rearrange them?

I   N   T   E   S   L

If you're like most people, you immediately saw "LISTEN." But what else do those letters spell? Look closely—do you see "SILENT" as well?

Interesting, isn't it, that those six letters, slightly rearranged, capture the essence of effective communication? In order to *really* listen, you must remain silent.

Of course, since communicating involves the *giving* as well as the *getting* of understanding, there is much more to communicating with a customer than simply listening actively. This chapter will examine a number of techniques for ensuring that those channels of understanding remain free-flowing and clear.

23

Remember the big power of little surprises.

When is the last time you received a thank-you note from someone you did business with? A real note, handwritten, two to three lines long and personally signed? Form letters, stamped cards, and even token follow-up "how'd we do?" forms abound, but real power lies in simple thank-you notes. They don't take long to complete, they're inexpensive, they show you care, and they tell customers that you're definitely not indifferent toward them. (Remember from Tip #8 why seven of ten customers go somewhere else?)

⌒ 24 ⌒

Learn the customer's name and use it frequently.

One of the most useful books ever written on service excellence was penned well over a half century ago. The most remarkable aspect of that remarkable little book is that it wasn't designed to improve customer service! Yet Dale Carnegie's *How to Win Friends and Influence People* continues to be a benchmark for practical hands-on, user-friendly service suggestions. Although the book brims with practical ideas for service excellence, one stands out above the rest: that you *learn and use the customer's name!*

Remember the television sitcom *Cheers?* Think of the places you go where you routinely hear your name used. Makes you feel good, doesn't it? Your customers will appreciate it just as much as you do when you're the customer.

25

Don't be afraid to ask "dumb" questions— and then to really listen to the answers.

Anyone who's been through military training probably remembers being told over and over that the only "dumb" question is the one you don't ask. Although that bit of advice may have seemed rather nonsensical at the time, any front-line duty you served subsequently, either in military service or customer service, probably consistently reinforced the wisdom of those words.

The best way to determine how to service, satisfy, and delight your customers is to find out how they want to be treated. And the fastest, most effective, foolproof way to do that is to ask. You can ask in person, on the phone, through surveys or focus groups—it doesn't matter. The important thing is to do it!

⌒ 26 ⌒

Create a "hot line" or other feedback system.

A terrific way to communicate is to capture solid feedback, perhaps through a special, dedicated telephone "hot line" your customers can use to ask questions, get current information, or reach service assistance. An 800 number is affordable for even the smallest companies, and it offers convenience and conveys an image of strength with large-market potential.

Surveying your customers' feelings about your organization can be a most insightful and effective way to gauge perceptions about your service levels. Survey formats are limited only by your imagination and the information you're trying to obtain. Here are a few suggestions for developing an effective survey:

- Provide a stamped, self-addressed mailer.

- Don't exceed one page in length.

- Personalize the survey with your logo or some other form of company identification.

- If practical, offer incentives (e.g., a discount on the next purchase, an opportunity to enter a drawing for a prize, a small gift).

- Make the majority of your questions multiple-choice, but provide two or three fill-ins (people with strong feelings will respond to narrative questions).

A sample survey form appears on page 43. Feel free to use it verbatim or as a model for developing your own.

A Sample Survey Model

HOW ARE WE DOING?

(Your logo, name, and address go here.)

Making your visit enjoyable and pleasant is our goal. Please take a moment to let us know how we're doing.

Our People	Excellent	Good	Average	Poor
Listened attentively to your concerns	☐	☐	☐	☐
Gave courteous, friendly service	☐	☐	☐	☐
Were helpful and knowledgeable	☐	☐	☐	☐
Had a professional manner and appearance	☐	☐	☐	☐
Our Facility				
Appeared neat and clean	☐	☐	☐	☐
Provided safe, easy access	☐	☐	☐	☐
Our Service Department				
Showed an understanding of your needs	☐	☐	☐	☐
Answered your questions satisfactorily	☐	☐	☐	☐
Delivered your job on schedule	☐	☐	☐	☐

Overall Yes No

Would you be willing to do business
  with us again? ☐ ☐

May we use you as a reference? ☐ ☐

How can we serve you better?

_____

_____

_____

_____

_____

What would you change about our operation?

_____

_____

_____

_____

Optional

Name: _____

Date: _____

Address: _____

Phone: _____

City/State: _____

Zip: _____

Develop a newsletter designed to entertain and inform your customers.

Not that many years ago, newsletters were an option available only to organizations with considerable in-house resources or the budget to use a newsletter service. Today an array of software is available to help you make a first-class impression on your customers. Remember that while it's perfectly fine to introduce a new product or service in your newsletter, the publication's primary function is to entertain, inform, and communicate with customers, not to sell.

☞ 28 ☜

Sponsor occasional focus groups of representative customers.

One of the most powerful yet infrequently used techniques for really communicating with customers is the focus group. This tool works effectively with both internal and external customers, though many organizations are reluctant to involve external customers because they assume they would be imposing. Actually, customers are usually flattered to be asked, and the message you send by asking is this: "We care about you, we value your input, and we perceive you as a partner in our business." Pretty good message to be sending, isn't it?

How does a focus group operate? In reality, it's just a one- to two-hour brainstorming session involving eight to twelve invited customers—internal, external, or both. The goal is to focus on a specific issue, such as improving the level of service you provide to your customers. Invariably, new and constructive ideas surface and communication channels are enhanced.

⌐ 29 ⌐

Invite customers to attend (or even better, lead!) a sales meeting.

Frequently when this technique is proposed, it's not well received. Why? "We don't want to give away secrets" is one often-cited reason, as is "I'd be embarrassed for them to see what goes on in there!"

Though both reactions are understandable, neither holds much water. If your sales meetings or your service meetings would be a source of embarrassment, you need to reevaluate the sessions anyway. It's unlikely that anything positive is being accomplished, and probably more harm than good is the result.

What about the possibility of giving away secrets? Certainly there are items that may be inappropriate to discuss in front of anyone outside your organization. Simply don't schedule such items for this type of meeting.

By the way, internal customers from other departments might also be great candidates to attend (or lead) your next meeting!

⌒ 30 ⌒

Create a mission statement that sparks enthusiasm.

In a gathering of business people, it's always gratifying to see the response when someone asks "How many of you have written mission statements for customer service?" Many hands go up. But when the follow-up question is posed—"How many of you know what that mission statement says?"—at least half the hands drop!

Although having a service mission statement is a good start toward providing service excellence, the document doesn't mean very much if it's just a hollow collection of words. You've seen those types of mission statements—they're framed in the lobby, they're emblazoned on the first page of the annual report, and yet they're in nobody's heart.

Much more important than having a mission statement for customer service is having a *customer service mission.* One represents words; the other represents everything discussed in this book.

A meaningful exercise you can try is to get your people together—by department, shift, floor, or however your team is organized—and ask this question: "What is our customer service mission?" Give everyone the opportunity to provide input, and then discuss the ideas and dissect them. Finally, mold them into a meaningful statement of your customer service mission.

Some examples follow:

- "Quality service means an unending devotion to creating pleasurable experiences for people." (the Disney Organization)

- "To be a catalyst in the development of black entrepreneurs." (Clark Atlanta University Business School)

- "Service is the only thing we don't make light of." (Georgia Lighting)

In customer service terms, what is your organization's reason for being?

_____

_____

_____

⌒ 31 ⌒

Make an occasional non-sales visit or phone call to "see how it's going."

A colleague once related how two of the nicest, most talented young girls in the neighborhood lived right next door to him, but he and his wife saw them only when the girls wanted to sell something—Girl Scout cookies, candy so the band could be in the Rose Bowl Parade, frozen pizza for new uniforms, coupon books for cheerleader equipment, and on and on. He got so that he winced whenever he saw one of them at the door.

One day he asked them, "Mary, Sarah, how come we see you two only when you have something to sell us?" A better relationship came out of that exchange, and he was more receptive to their occasional "selling" visits.

How often do your customers, when visited or called by somebody from your company, say to themselves, "Mary, Sarah, how come we see you only...?" Think about the other ways you can stay in touch with your customers.

32

Be visible—community involvement and exposure are powerful positive communicators.

Becoming involved with local charities, community events, and philanthropic activities often benefits not only the community and those directly served, but also the participants and their organizations. Certainly the motivation in giving to the community is not to enrich yourself or your company, but isn't it one of the happy quirks of life that such enrichment inevitably occurs?

There are also a number of non-giving ways to gain positive visibility for your organization in the community, including attending networking events or writing articles on service or about your industry for local publications. Another effective technique for positively positioning yourself and your organization is to address civic clubs and special interest groups at their luncheon and dinner meetings. This puts a "face" on your business and adds dimension to your service commitment.

⌒ 33 ⌒

Remember that everything—vehicles, ads, stationery, cards, people—conveys an image.

An over-the-road trucking firm needed to hire a truck-washing service, so the fleet manager began his search in the yellow pages. One ad in particular attracted his attention—the one for "Sparkle Klean." A couple of things came up, however, so the manager decided to wait until Monday morning to call. Over the weekend the manager saw a "Sparkle Klean" truck on the road—and it was anything but "Klean." In fact, it was filthy! He did hire a truck-washing company on Monday, but it certainly wasn't "Sparkle Klean."

The point here is that everything conveys an image about your organization. Company vehicles, how they're driven, employee appearance, business cards, *everything* contributes to a customer's (or potential customer's) perception. Remember, *perception* is reality in the marketplace.

ᗌ 34 ᗍ

Keep customers current on industry and market trends.

As mentioned earlier, newsletters are an effective vehicle
for presenting what's new and of interest to your
customer. But there are other ways to keep your
customers informed! When you learn of something that
might be of interest to a certain client, pass it along the
next time that person's in, or take a minute to convey the
information with a personal call. This technique, though
informal, is effective. Remember, most of the customers
you lose leave because they feel you're indifferent to
them. But there's no way they could feel that way if you
routinely employ this technique.

⌒ 35 ⌒

Develop profiles on your customers and send them relevant announcements, articles, and so on.

This technique has proven very valuable to firms that use it. It's easy, it's fun, it's inexpensive, and it works! Simply keep a written or computerized record of dates, people, and events of importance to your customers. Things like family members' names, hobbies, favorite teams, interests, and so forth. When something about them, their family, their business, or their interests appears, cut it out and send it along. It's a terrific way to say you really do care.

⌒ 36 ⌒

Make understanding your customers
a priority—not the other way around.

Do you remember the definition of communication that
came up earlier —"the giving and getting of
understanding"? This definition prioritizes the order in
which you should give and get understanding—and it's
the hallmark of the truly exceptional service provider.

⊂ 37 ⊃

Encourage employee involvement and feedback.

By this point, you're a believer in the power of involving *everyone* in the service function, right? As discussed previously, internal customer focus groups are one way to achieve such involvement. Another potentially powerful tool for encouraging involvement is a suggestion system. Though such a system can be as simple or as complex as you'd like, simplicity has very strong merits.

The Employee Involvement Association (formerly the National Association of Suggestion Systems) estimates there are approximately six thousand formal suggestion programs in the United States and at least that many semiformal ones. Here are some tips the Employee Involvement Association offers for a successful suggestion system:

- Enlist the support of top management.
- Lay out the goals the program should achieve.
- Be sure managers and supervisors are receptive to ideas from others.
- Designate an individual or committee to administer the program.
- Set up an awards schedule for the best suggestions and stick with it.
- Inform employees about the suggestion program in writing, explaining how it works and how they can benefit from it.

- Publicize the program often.
- Respond promptly to each suggestion, whether it's adopted or not.
- Keep accurate records of all suggestions to ensure proper awarding of prizes.
- Have a company officer present the awards.

☞ 38 ☜

Beware of "WAD IT W!"

Give up? "WAD IT W!" is an acronym for those six paralyzing words that prevent so many organizations from taking their service to the next level—*"We've always done it this way!"* Of all the reasons for doing, or not doing, something in customer service, this is the worst. In the world of customer service, it pays to get bold, get creative, and get innovative!

Now, you may be saying, "Get real!" but the reality is that in today's marketplace you need to be willing to take risks. Not big risks necessarily, but you must be willing to try new approaches, to evaluate new techniques, to be somewhat different. Here are a few examples of some little things that are making big differences for many companies:

- Supply business cards for *all* employees. The heightened feeling of self-esteem and sense of belonging to the team this generates can be fantastic.

- Provide professional name badges (first name only is fine) for everyone with external customer contact.

- Carry a supply of cards, literature, and information about the organization with you at all times and distribute it freely.

- Have a casual day or dress down day. *The Wall Street Journal* recently reported that fifteen of the top twenty Fortune 500 companies are now doing this every Friday.

Find any surprises in this list? Shake up your thinking at all?

39

Be extremely aware of your telephone technique.

Ever hear the expression, "I shot myself in the foot"?
Probably not literally—but figuratively—thousands of
people shoot themselves in the foot every day, and the
telephone is the weapon of choice!

The telephone impacts your customers' perception of
your business more than any other single tool you use.
You can use it to delight them or send them running to
the competition—the choice is yours!

Books have been written on the proper use of the
telephone. Seminars are conducted every day on effective
telephone technique. Audiocassettes are available to help
you be more phone proficient. Despite this deluge of
advice and instruction, many in customer service appear
to have no idea how to use the telephone effectively.

Here are some suggestions to help you come across as a
real telephone "pro" every time you lift the receiver (or
activate your headset!):

For outgoing calls

- Plan the call. Invest a few seconds to jot down a mini-
  agenda.

- Smile when you speak. People really can hear the
  smile in your voice.

- Identify yourself early.

- If you're leaving a recorded message, speak slowly,
  repeat your name and number, and leave a specific
  message.

- Hang up last (wait for the "click").

For incoming calls

- Smile when you speak. (It's not a bad idea to keep a small mirror handy.)

- Have paper, pencil, and a calendar nearby.

- Avoid eating, drinking, or smoking while on the phone.

- Use a complete greeting (salutation, organizational I.D., personal I.D., offer to assist [optional]). For example: "Good morning. Computer Care. This is Roy. How may I help you?"

- Use the caller's name.

- Take complete messages.

- Hang up last.

Why hang up last? Because the other person may have a last-minute addition to the conversation that you may otherwise miss. The only way to know that you're hanging up last is to wait for the "click."

40

Strive to answer the phone on the second or third ring.

This telephone technique is so important that it deserves to stand apart from the others. Have you ever called a business and endured the phone ringing seven, eight, nine, or more times? Depending on why you're calling, that can be infuriating. And it certainly creates an unprofessional image for the business. Yet it happens countless times every day.

Answering the phone on no later than the third ring conveys a positive and professional image. If for some reason the phone does ring five or more times, try saying "I'm sorry for the delay" as a substitute for the "salutation" part of your greeting.

Having explored behaviors, attitudes, and communication techniques—the B-A-C part of getting customers to come BACK—it's on to the *knowledge* component, covered in Chapter 4.

Chapter Four

Knowledge Required to Delight

*"People don't care how much you know
until they know how much you care."*

Today providing customer service, even excellent customer service, is not enough; just about any competitor you have is capable of doing that. Until recently, businesses thought that customer *satisfaction* should be the goal. Well, that's been superseded too; in today's competitive environment, even *satisfaction* isn't enough—you must *delight* your customers.

Here's an example:

Bonnie drives a company car and is responsible for regular routine maintenance. For several years, a local quick lubrication facility took care of that for her. The company's *service* was always impeccable—the staff checked fluid levels, followed proper procedures, and used quality products. However, Bonnie never felt real *satisfaction* with their work; she was seldom greeted properly, they never bothered to learn her name, and a sincere "thank you" was rare indeed. She therefore was happy to discover that a new quick lubrication operation was opening nearby. It took only one visit to learn that this place knew about customer satisfaction. The quality of service easily equaled that of the other place, plus they added a cheery greeting, used her name regularly, and genuinely conveyed that they appreciated her business.

The second visit, however, really pushed her over the top. The team did a superb job of service, used all the techniques to ensure *satisfaction*, but then moved into the realm of customer *delight*—they vacuumed her car!

Satisfying customers is important, but if you're going to keep them coming back, you need to know what will delight them.

⌐ 41 ⌐

Spend time at the front line—let customers and employees see you caring.

If you're an owner, manager, supervisor, or boss of any kind, get out and get among 'em! Remember, let everyone see that you are committed to *customer service,* not just *lip service.* The phenomenally successful Marriott organization personifies this approach—it's not unusual to find one of the Marriotts roaming the hotel restaurant asking customers what they think of the service, or manning the phones at the front desk, learning firsthand what guests are thinking.

⌒ 42 ⌒

Learn all you can about your products, service, and industry.

In some cases, having *complete* product knowledge would literally be impossible—your company may have far too many products or services to be familiar with them all. You must, however, know how to bring the information and the customer together.

Here's an example of what happens when you don't:

A couple was searching for a new television. After some shopping around, the couple decided to visit a nationally known retailer, where floor-to-ceiling televisions covered all four walls. No salespeople seemed particularly moved to be of service, but after comparing the various sets available, the couple found two of interest within their price range. After happening on a sales associate wandering around with a thick looseleaf binder, the couple queried her concerning the televisions' differences. She responded: *"The one on the bottom is cheaper."* When the couple pressed for more information about picture clarity, warranty, and other specifics, she crossed her arms, sighed deeply, and said, "You know, people ask me that all the time"—end of discussion.

Now no one certainly would have expected this associate to know all the different features of all those televisions, but don't you think if she had been asked that question even *once* before, she should have an answer? Or she could have responded like this: "That's a great question— let's look in this book and find out together." (She never did open her binder.) Needless to say, the couple didn't buy a television there!

43

Learn all you can about your customers' products, services, and businesses.

Of all the important lessons you can learn concerning serving, satisfying, and delighting the customer, the one that consistently yields the greatest results is to be accepted by customers as a partner in their businesses. When you can position yourself as one who knows their businesses as well as they do, customers' levels of trust, confidence, and delight skyrocket.

⌒ 44 ⌒

Don't be afraid to recommend a competitor if you can't meet a need.

Companies with enough confidence in their quality and level of service to unhesitatingly refer a potential customer elsewhere convey two very strong messages. First, these companies give the impression of *really* having the customer's interest at the forefront of their philosophy. Second, they demonstrate unwavering confidence in their ability to delight the customer on occasions when they *can* provide the product or service required.

45

Do business with your customers as a customer of theirs.

This has nothing to do with itchy backs! The old saying, "You scratch my back, I'll scratch yours" really doesn't have a place in the vocabulary of a true customer service professional—it implies that you make decisions based solely on relationships without regard to the quality of service involved. This doesn't mean that relationships aren't important (they are incredibly so), but both parties need to target delighting the other without individual gain as a motive.

◌ 46 ◌

Use "mystery shoppers" to gauge true customer feelings.

Mystery shoppers aren't people who walk into a business with large paper bags on their heads, trying very hard not to be noticed. Actually, the exact opposite is true— mystery shoppers want very much to be noticed! In fact, that's why they're there in the first place—the way they're treated is probably a pretty good indicator of what all customers encounter.

There are consultants all over the country who will gladly accept thousands of your organization's dollars to "mystery shop" the organization. That expenditure, however, is totally unnecessary. All it takes to effectively find out how your organization is treating your customers is to get someone the associates aren't familiar with (someone from another branch, a friend, etc.), determine what it is you want to gauge, and then decide how to track what you've found out.

If you'd like to try using mystery shoppers to help ensure that your customers keep coming BACK, the charts on the following pages contain questions regarding *behaviors, attitudes, communication techniques,* and *knowledge* you may want feedback on.

For Mystery Shoppers Who Visit in Person

The Greeting

Were you met with an actual greeting? _____

Were you made to feel welcome? How? _____

Were you smiled at? _____

Did the associate use a pleasant tone of voice? _____

Service

Were you treated courteously and in a friendly way? _____

Did you receive prompt attention? _____

Did the associate introduce himself or herself? _____

Did you receive an offer of assistance? _____

What was it? _____

If you made a purchase, were you thanked properly? _____

How? _____

Knowledge

Were the personnel knowledgeable? _____

Were the personnel able to answer your questions? _____

Were the personnel willing to help find the answers to your
questions if they didn't know them? _____

Were the personnel able to find the answers to your questions
in a timely manner? _____

Exit

Did someone thank you for visiting? _____

Were you invited back? _____

Briefly describe your overall experience:

_____

For Mystery Shoppers Who Call on the Phone

The Greeting

How many times did the phone ring? _____

Could you understand the greeting? _____

What was it? _____

What was the greeter's voice tone? _____

The Conversation

Were you put on hold? _____

What words were used to do that? _____

How long did you hold? _____

Were you checked on at twenty- to thirty-second intervals? ___
_____

Were you thanked for holding? _____

Could you hear a smile in the employee's voice? _____
_____

Was the employee eating? _____ drinking? _____
smoking?_____

The Attitude

Did the person seem willing to help? _____

Did you feel your call was appreciated? _____

What was your overall impression of the call?

_____

_____

_____

Be proactive, not reactive, to change in the marketplace.

The only absolute, guaranteed, sure bet in the wonderful world of delighting the customer is that change has become the only constant! The good news is that you can choose your response to that change. You can be proactive by staying on top of customer needs and expectations, or you can travel the reactive road. Your choice of which road you select, *proactive* or *reactive*, will determine whether you eventually find yourself in the sleepy little town called *Inactive*, or in the bustling metropolis of *Success!*

⌒ 48 ⌒

"Customers don't care how much you know until they know how much you care."

It the above quote looks familiar, it's because it bears repeating! The essence of delighting your customers is to genuinely care for their well-being. The old saying, "Knowledge is power" isn't exactly true—to be more precise, *applied knowledge* is power. You may have a broader knowledge and a deeper understanding than anyone else alive about what it takes to delight the customer, but unless you can apply that knowledge in a way that demonstrates you care, the knowledge itself holds little real value.

Having examined this final component—knowledge—the next step is to assimilate all you've learned about superior customer service and develop an action plan.

Chapter Five

Putting It All Together

"Right or wrong, the customer is always right."
—Marshall Field

*A*pproaching your role as a service professional with the realization that although customers aren't always right, they're always customers is what this book has been about. Certainly you have encountered, and will continue to encounter, some customers who delight you when they take their business elsewhere! But in the vast majority of cases, you want your customers to remain your own.

The preceding tips and techniques are offered to help you achieve that goal—to keep them coming BACK to you. If you do nothing different, if you change nothing about your current delivery of service, then nothing will change. Nothing will improve. How can it?

Map out your journey to the ultimate level of service excellence—delighting the customer—by completing the action plan that follows. Complete it thoughtfully, even involve your team, and then accept congratulations in advance on the successful care and keeping of your customers. Remember to consider all the elements of BACK as you create your plan.

Customer Service Action Plan

A. There are many new creative, maybe even risky, things you can do to keep your customers coming BACK—what are they? Use the BACK model to brainstorm.

Behaviors:

_____

_____

_____

_____

_____

Attitudes:

_____

_____

_____

_____

Communication Techniques:

_____

_____

_____

_____

Knowledge:

_____

_____

_____

_____

_____

B. Now analyze the ideas you brainstormed in Part A. Which ones could you actually implement?

By this time next month, I will:

_____

_____

_____

By the end of next quarter, I will:

_____

_____

_____

During the next six months, I will:

_____

_____

_____

By this time next year, I will:

_____

_____

_____

Bibliography and Suggested Resources

Books

Albrecht, Karl, and Ron Zemke. *Service America!: Doing Business in the New Economy.* Homewood, IL: Dow Jones-Irwin, 1985.

Berry, Leonard L. *Great Service: A Framework for Action.* New York: The Free Press, 1995.

Carlson, Jan. *Moments of Truth.* Cambridge, MS: Ballinger, 1987.

Carnegie, Dale. *How to Win Friends and Influence People*. New York: Simon & Schuster, 1981.

Connellan, Thomas K., and Ron Zemke. *Sustaining Knock Your Socks Off Service*. New York: Amacom, 1993.

Covey, Stephen R. *The Seven Habits of Highly Effective People*. New York: Simon & Schuster, 1989.

Friedman, Paul. *How to Deal With Difficult People*. Mission, KS: SkillPath Publications, 1991.

Glen, Peter. *It's Not My Department: How to Get the Service You Want, Exactly the Way You Want It!* New York: Morrow, 1990.

Liswood, Laura A. *Serving Them Right: Innovative and Powerful Customer Retention Strategies*. New York: Harper & Row, 1990.

Rosenbluth, Hal F., and Diane McFerrin Peters. *The Customer Comes Second: And Other Secrets of Exceptional Service*. New York: William Morrow, 1994.

Sewell, Carl. *Customers for Life: How to Turn That One-Time Buyer Into a Lifetime Customer*. New York: Doubleday, 1990.

Temme, Jim. *Total Quality Customer Service*. Mission, KS: SkillPath Publications, 1994.

Trimble, Vance H. *Sam Walton: The Inside Story of America's Richest Man*. New York: Dutton, 1990.

Woolf, Bob. *Friendly Persuasion: My Life as a Negotiator*. New York: Putnam, 1990.

Audiocassettes

Fracassi, Linda. *How to Provide Excellent Customer Service.* Mission, KS: SkillPath Publications, 1989.

Lantz, Roy. *The Care and Keeping of Customers.* Marietta, GA: Human Resource Dynamics, 1991.

Available From SkillPath Publications

Self-Study Sourcebooks

Climbing the Corporate Ladder: What You Need to Know and Do to Be a Promotable Person *by Barbara Pachter and Marjorie Brody*

Coping With Supervisory Nightmares: 12 Common Nightmares of Leadership and What You Can Do About Them *by Michael and Deborah Singer Dobson*

Defeating Procrastination: 52 Fail-Safe Tips for Keeping Time on Your Side *by Marlene Caroselli, Ed.D.*

Discovering Your Purpose *by Ivy Haley*

Going for the Gold: Winning the Gold Medal for Financial Independence *by Lesley D. Bissett, CFP*

Having Something to Say When You Have to Say Something: The Art of Organizing Your Presentation *by Randy Horn*

Info-Flood: How to Swim in a Sea of Information Without Going Under *by Marlene Caroselli, Ed.D.*

The Innovative Secretary *by Marlene Caroselli, Ed.D.*

Letters & Memos: Just Like That! *by Dave Davies*

Mastering the Art of Communication: Your Keys to Developing a More Effective Personal Style *by Michelle Fairfield Poley*

Obstacle Illusions: Coverting Crisis to Opportunity *by Marlene Caroselli, Ed.D.*

Organized for Success! 95 Tips for Taking Control of Your Time, Your Space, and Your Life *by Nanci McGraw*

A Passion to Lead! How to Develop Your Natural Leadership Ability *by Michael Plumstead*

P.E.R.S.U.A.D.E.: Communication Strategies That Move People to Action *by Marlene Caroselli, Ed.D.*

Productivity Power: 250 Great Ideas for Being More Productive *by Jim Temme*

Promoting Yourself: 50 Ways to Increase Your Prestige, Power, and Paycheck *by Marlene Caroselli, Ed.D.*

Proof Positive: How to Find Errors Before They Embarrass You *by Karen L. Anderson*

Risk-Taking: 50 Ways to Turn Risks Into Rewards *by Marlene Caroselli, Ed.D. and David Harris*

Stress Control: How You Can Find Relief From Life's Daily Stress *by Steve Bell*

The Technical Writer's Guide *by Robert McGraw*

Total Quality Customer Service: How to Make It Your Way of Life *by Jim Temme*

Write It Right! A Guide for Clear and Correct Writing *by Richard Andersen and Helene Hinis*

Your Total Communication Image *by Janet Signe Olson, Ph.D.*

Handbooks

The ABC's of Empowered Teams: Building Blocks for Success *by Mark Towers*

Assert Yourself! Developing Power-Packed Communication Skills to Make Your Points Clearly, Confidently, and Persuasively *by Lisa Contini*

Breaking the Ice: How to Improve Your On-the-Spot Communication Skills *by Deborah Shouse*

The Care and Keeping of Customers: A Treasury of Facts, Tips, and Proven Techniques for Keeping Your Customers Coming BACK! *by Roy Lantz*

Challenging Change: Five Steps for Dealing With Change *by Holly DeForest and Mary Steinberg*

Dynamic Delegation: A Manager's Guide for Active Empowerment *by Mark Towers*

Every Woman's Guide to Career Success *by Denise M. Dudley*

Exploring Personality Styles: A Guide for Better Understanding Yourself and Your Colleagues *by Michael Dobson*

Grammar? No Problem! *by Dave Davies*

Great Openings and Closings: 28 Ways to Launch and Land Your Presentations With Punch, Power, and Pizazz *by Mari Pat Varga*

Hiring and Firing: What Every Manager Needs to Know *by Marlene Caroselli, Ed.D. with Laura Wyeth, Ms.Ed.*

How to Be a More Effective Group Communicator: Finding Your Role and Boosting Your Confidence in Group Situations *by Deborah Shouse*

How to Deal With Difficult People *by Paul Friedman*

Learning to Laugh at Work: The Power of Humor in the Workplace *by Robert McGraw*

Making Your Mark: How to Develop a Personal Marketing Plan for Becoming More Visible and More Appreciated at Work *by Deborah Shouse*

Meetings That Work *by Marlene Caroselli, Ed.D.*

The Mentoring Advantage: How to Help Your Career Soar to New Heights *by Pam Grout*

Minding Your Business Manners: Etiquette Tips for Presenting Yourself Professionally in Every Business Situation *by Marjorie Brody and Barbara Pachter*

Misspeller's Guide *by Joel and Ruth Schroeder*

Motivation in the Workplace: How to Motivate Workers to Peak Performance and Productivity *by Barbara Fielder*

NameTags Plus: Games You Can Play When People Don't Know What to Say *by Deborah Shouse*

Networking: How to Creatively Tap Your People Resources *by Colleen Clarke*

New & Improved! 25 Ways to Be More Creative and More Effective *by Pam Grout*

Power Write! A Practical Guide to Words That Work *by Helene Hinis*

The Power of Positivity: Eighty ways to energize your life *by Joel and Ruth Schroeder*

Putting Anger to Work For You *by Ruth and Joel Schroeder*

Reinventing Your Self: 28 Strategies for Coping With Change *by Mark Towers*

Saying "No" to Negativity: How to Manage Negativity in Yourself, Your Boss, and Your Co-Workers *by Zoie Kaye*

The Supervisor's Guide: The Everyday Guide to Coordinating People and Tasks *by Jerry Brown and Denise Dudley, Ph.D.*

Taking Charge: A Personal Guide to Managing Projects and Priorities *by Michal E. Feder*

Treasure Hunt: 10 Stepping Stones to a New and More Confident You! *by Pam Grout*

A Winning Attitude: How to Develop Your Most Important Asset! *by Michelle Fairfield Poley*

For more information, call 1-800-873-7545.

Notes

Notes

Notes

Notes

Notes

Notes